SCIENCE

Customized Problem-Solving Strategies

PEARSON

ISBN 13: 978-0-7854-6643-7
ISBN 10:   0-7854-6643-6
5 6 7 8 9 10 V036 15 14 13 12 11 10

1-800-992-0244
www.pearson.com

CONTENTS

What Is the AMP MATH SYSTEM?

The AMP Math System is an innovative math intervention program for middle- and high-school students who are struggling to connect and apply what they have been taught in their mathematics classes.

Based on the Curriculum Focal Points for Prekindergarten through Grade 8 Mathematics: A Quest for Coherence (NCTM 2006), the AMP Math System teaches six focal points in each level. A focal point is a core mathematical structure that spans skills and concepts typically taught at various grade levels. Built on focal points, the AMP Math System lays a conceptual foundation that facilitates deep mathematical understanding and fluency.

More and more students are arriving in middle and high school unprepared for the challenges they face, both in the classroom and in the future. The AMP Math System gives students, teachers, and schools the confidence and skill to achieve their maximum potential. The AMP Math System combines research-based strategies with high-interest, student-selected topics.

THE AMP MATH SYSTEM—FOCUSING ON KEY MATHEMATICAL TOPICS AND PROBLEM-SOLVING STRATEGIES.

Based on the NCTM Curriculum Focal Points

- Each unit in the program addresses one focal point in depth in the context of associated concepts, skills, and applications.

- Lessons emphasize communication, reasoning, representation, connections, and problem solving.

- The instructional model encourages students to think mathematically and prepares them to solve many problems that they will face in the future in both the classroom and the workplace.

Incorporates Problem-Solving Strategies

- Six problem-solving strategies are explicitly taught and applied in the AMP Math System.

- The first unit in the program introduces the problem-solving strategies and the remaining units expand on each strategy, encouraging students to choose a strategy and apply it to solve a problem.

- Units utilize a systematic instructional routine that includes whole class instruction, guided practice, and discussion.

Provides Context for Problem-Solving and Comprehension

- Units in the AMP Math System have corresponding project magazines that explore real life mathematical concepts and challenges in student-selected topic areas.

- Students read from the project magazines almost every day in order to build background knowledge plus communication and reasoning skills.

- Units also include reading strategies, taught one at a time, that support student learning by helping them understand what they read and enabling them to connect problem-solving strategies to the math skills they are acquiring.

HOW DOES THE AMP MATH SYSTEM SUPPORT THE CONTENT AREAS?

THE CHALLENGE

- Students who are performing significantly below grade level in mathematics may have trouble applying math or problem-solving skills to other subject areas such as science and social studies.

- Students who are not comfortable with math may struggle in other content areas.

- In their classes, teachers trained in science and social studies may encounter students who have math anxiety or who perform poorly in math. This affects students' work in content-area classes, but content-area teachers may not have the math background or tools to help these students.

THE AMP MATH SYSTEM SOLUTION

Customized problem-solving strategies are delivered directly to content-area teachers.

The focus is on expository text in the AMP Link Magazines and the Student Guide passages. In their AMP Math System class, students are learning problem-solving strategies and math vocabulary that they can directly apply to their content-area texts to help them learn. The Customized Problem-Solving Strategies books and the AMP Math System class materials support the content areas:

Customized Problem-Solving Strategies

- guide content-area teachers to support and apply the problem-solving strategies.

- clearly explain each problem-solving strategy.

- give content-area teachers specific suggestions for implementing the strategies.

- supply blackline masters with directions for students to apply the strategies to their content-area textbooks.

- enable students to strengthen problem-solving skills while increasing their knowledge and understanding of content.

- provide options scripting for explaining the strategies to students.

- offer ideas for applying vocabulary and fluency learning to content-area classes.

The AMP Math System Class Materials

- present informational reading passages and problem-solving scenarios that have textbook-like headings, formats, visuals, and captions.

- include AMP Link Magazines that are mainly nonfiction and expose students to the expository text structures they encounter in their content-area reading.

- provide each unit's vocabulary as a master list for use in all curriculum areas. (Ask the math teacher for a copy from the Teacher's Edition.)

A COMPLETE MATH INTERVENTION SYSTEM

Instruction: Explicit and systematic student and teacher materials.

Content Area Support: Mathematical and problem-solving instruction is carried over into other subjects as problem-solving strategies are reinforced by content-area teachers.

Professional Development: Ongoing support helps math and content-area teachers become comfortable and adept at teaching math and problem-solving.

INTENSE
SKILLS
INSTRUCTION

CONTENT-AREA
TEACHER
SUPPORT

PROFESSIONAL
DEVELOPMENT

Using the Six Problem-Solving Strategies

What role can a science teacher play?

Students often need help applying strategies and knowledge from one subject area to another. Your involvement in helping them transfer problem-solving strategies to science will benefit both you and your students.

You can help students apply problem-solving strategies to the materials in your class. First, familiarize yourself with the Four-Step Problem-Solving Plan and with the summary of each strategy in this book. Then model each strategy for students, using your class textbook or other material. Use the blackline masters that accompany each strategy to reinforce the strategy and to help your students apply it to science assignments.

What are the problem-solving strategies?

The AMP Math System introduces students to problem-solving with the Four-Step Problem-Solving Plan:

Read

Plan

Solve

Check

Problem-solving strategies in the AMP Math System include:

Draw a Picture or Use a Model

Drawing a picture can help students visualize and better understand problems. As students read text or encounter a problem, they can make a visual representation of what they read.

Using a model can also help students visualize problems. Students can either create a physical model or a model on paper to represent what they read.

For example, students learning about atoms and molecules might find it useful to draw a picture of the parts of an atom or to make a physical model of a molecule.

Find a Pattern

Finding a pattern can help students solve problems in which numbers or objects repeat or change in a predictable way. To use this strategy, students look at the numbers carefully and identify how they change to determine the "rule" of the pattern. With numbers, the rule might be to "subtract three from the previous number" or to "multiply the previous number by 5."

Students in science classes may encounter patterns when studying weather, nature, temperature, or chemistry, for example.

Make a List

Students can make lists in order to see information in an organized way. Lists can help students keep track of possible combinations of items or outcomes of situations.

Science classes often require students to learn and manage a lot of new information and data. Students can make organized lists to process and understand data.

Try a Simpler Form of the Problem

Often, students are confronted with a difficult or complicated problem. Students can use what they already know about a part of the problem. Students could also use simpler numbers to help them solve a complicated problem.

Working with very large numbers or with complicated chemical formulas are parts of learning about science. This strategy gives students a way to simplify difficult problems.

Make a Table or a Chart

Just as students can make lists in order to organize information, they can make tables or charts to organize and display information. Tables and charts can also be used to find patterns.

Science students may be asked to work with large amounts of data, to compare and contrast items, or to classify items. Making a table or a chart can help them solve problems that involve these skills.

Guess, Check, and Revise

Students can use the guess, check, and revise strategy to make a logical guess about the answer to a problem, check their work, and revise their answer as necessary.

Many situations in science require an educated guess followed by revisions of that guess until arriving at a correct, or the correct answer.

Developing Your Students' Math Vocabulary

How important is math vocabulary?

For students to have confidence in solving math problems they encounter in other subject areas, they need to have a familiarity with math vocabulary. If students do not understand or are intimidated by vocabulary, they may have a hard time solving the problem even if they possess the necessary skills.

What can science teachers do?

Use the ideas here to (1) support students' vocabulary learning in their math classes and (2) teach the terms students need for success in science.

Reinforce the vocabulary students are learning in the AMP Math System.

The AMP Math System includes both math vocabulary and content-area vocabulary. The math vocabulary includes academic words essential to comprehending mathematics. The content-area vocabulary includes academic words found in other content areas such as science, social studies, art, etc. Ask the AMP Math System teacher for the unit word lists (they are blackline masters in the back of the Teacher's Edition).

* Use the words in your class discussions where applicable.

* Incorporate the words in the questions you ask in class.

* Occasionally, call attention to your use of the words.

Explicitly teach the vocabulary in your textbook.

Research shows that the most effective point at which to teach these words is before students encounter them—at the beginning of a unit or chapter. Avoid sending students to a dictionary or relying on glossary definitions. Students need real-world explanations with plenty of examples.

Below is one routine for introducing students to the vocabulary they will need:

1. Present the list on the board or with handouts.

2. Go over the list orally with students. Ask them to say each word with you until the whole class is saying each word loudly and clearly. Repeating the words is a first step in having students feel comfortable and confident with them.

3. Provide a brief explanation of each word. Personalize the words as much as possible. Below are examples of student-friendly explanations:
   • If an object or event is **monumental,** it is huge or important.
   • A **majority** is more than half of the people or things in a group.
   • When you **classify** things, you sort them. You put them into groups of things that are alike.

4. Follow up each explanation with an example:
   • Planning the club project was a **monumental** task.
   • In a school of 100 students, 51 or more students are a **majority.**
   • Scientists **classify** different tornado winds by the kind of damage they cause.

5. Ask students questions that personalize the words.
   • What **monumental** historic event has happened in your lifetime?
   • How do you spend the **majority** of your time?
   • What are some ways you could **classify** movies?

Ask students to sort the words.

Students can work in pairs with sets of about 10 words on small cards or slips of paper.

Some teachers ask students to come up with their own classifications. You may be surprised at how creative and adept your students can be at this activity. Challenge them to come up with a category no one else in the class will have thought of. Additionally or alternatively, give them categories related to the theme or topic the class is studying.

Follow up by asking a pair of students for their categories, finding out who else in the class used the same ones, and having them tell the words in the category. Encourage discussion, challenges, and additions.

Make word webs.

Draw a circle on the board and write the word in the circle. Draw spokes and circles surrounding it. Have students generate related words for the outer circles. The words can be related by topic; they can be other forms of the word; or they can be simple associations.

Ask for examples and NON-examples.

Students enjoy the process of explaining what the word does *not* refer to.
NON-examples are a powerful means of clarifying understanding of the word or term.

For the word monumental
Examples:
high school graduation
signing of the Declaration of Independence
discovery of penicillin

NON-examples:
going to the grocery store
taking a shower
watching television

Ask students to draw a picture.

As students decide how to visually represent the meaning of a word, they gain a
deeper understanding of its meaning. This can be challenging. Have students work
in pairs to come up with concepts and drawings.

Ask students to associate new words with known words.

This technique helps them assimilate the new words more quickly. Discuss synonyms
and antonyms. Ask them to list other, more familiar words in the word family. Use
analogies. Ask, *How would you connect these two words? What do these words
have in common? How are these words alike and different?*

Teach and use context clues.

As students look in the text for clues to a word's meaning, they are taking an active
approach in the discovery of meaning. Questions to prompt contextualizing include:
*What can you tell about the word from this sentence? How does the sentence help
you understand the meaning of the word? What clues in the sentence help you
figure out the word?*

Analyze the word.

Have students look for prefixes and suffixes. Help them identify the base word or a
familiar root such as *port*, meaning "carry," in *transport* and *export*. Point out words
with multiple meanings such as the differences between the noun and verb definition
of *factor*. It's possible that students know one meaning of a word, but not the
meaning for the way the word is being used in your class.

Transfer, extend, and reinforce the use of vocabulary words.

Encourage students to use the words in their everyday speaking and writing, in
their class discussions, and in their class writing assignments. Questions to prompt
transferring include: *How often did you use _____ or hear someone else
using _____ today?*

Draw a Picture or Use a Model

Drawing a picture can help students visualize and better understand problems. As students read text or encounter a problem, they can make a visual representation of what they read.

Using a model can also help students visualize problems. Students can either create a physical model or a model on paper to represent what they read.

Here are some ways you can help your students apply the Four-Step Problem-Solving Plan with the Draw a Picture or Use a Model strategy to solve problems in science class.

1 Read

Students should read the problem to discover what information they are to gather. Students should study the problem to decide if they have all the information they need, and then begin thinking about the steps needed to solve the problem.

2 Plan

Students should think about the steps they will need to do to solve the problem. They will make a plan and lay out each step.

3 Solve

Students follow their plan to solve the problem.

4 Check

Students check their work and reread the problem to see if their answer makes sense.

Samples of how Draw a Picture or Use a Model can be used in science:

• After students have read about the planets in the solar system, they may be asked which planets are furthest away or which are closest to the sun. Students might make a scale model to visualize how far each planet in the solar system is from the sun.

• Students learn about the Fahrenheit scale and the Celsius scale in physical science. Students might find it helpful to draw a picture of each temperature scale in order to compare boiling points and freezing points.

Applying the Strategy: Draw a Picture or Use a Model

Here are some tips for helping students apply this strategy before, during, and after they solve problems:

Before Students Solve

- **Explain the strategy.** Say, *Drawing a picture or using a model can help you visualize information. When you have a picture or model of the information, you can better understand and answer the problem.*

- **Model how to draw a picture.** Choose a science problem to solve. Say, *To solve this problem, drawing a picture can help me see what I am being asked and what I need to do to solve the problem. I take the information from the problem and use it to draw a picture. In this problem...* (State the main question the problem is asking and the details that are necessary to solve it.)

- **Evaluate a science problem with students.** Have students read a problem from their textbook and retell it in their own words. Next have them suggest how drawing a picture or using a model might help them understand the information in the problem and solve it. (Copy and distribute page 14 as a guide to help students with this strategy.)

As Students Solve

- **Have students check their understanding.** Direct students to stop periodically and ask themselves if they understand the problem they are working on. Have students identify the important information from the problem they use in their pictures or models.

- **Have students explain their pictures or models.** Ask volunteers to restate in their own words the main question the problem is asking and then have them explain the picture they drew or the model they made. Have them tell how the picture or model helped them understand and solve the problem, so that students who are struggling can make a connection between the drawing or model and how to solve the problem.

- **Have students check their work.** Then ask them to explain why their answer is correct.

- **If students' answers are not correct, have them reread the problem and make sure their drawing or model is accurate.** Help students use the information in their drawing or model to get the correct answer.

Using the Blackline Masters

Students can use the blackline master on page 14 to practice the Draw a Picture or Use a Model strategy to help them solve problems. Have them use the blackline master on page 15 to practice the strategy with the Four-Step Problem-Solving Plan. Copy and distribute one or both blackline masters. Guide students through each part.

Draw a Picture or Use a Model
(page 14)

Before You Solve

- Provide students with a problem from a science text. Direct students to read the problem.

- Have students answer the question on the blackline master and review their responses.

As You Solve

- Review the directions for the As You Solve chart.

- Guide students to identify the question being asked and important information in the problem. Have students tell whether they would draw a picture or use a model, and have them explain how this will help them solve the problem.

- Encourage students to copy the chart to help them solve other problems.

After You Solve

- Discuss the completed charts. Have students share their pictures or models and tell how they solved the problem.

- Explain that although some pictures or models may differ from each other, they all contain the same important details from the problem.

- Have students respond to the After You Solve question and discuss.

The Four-Step Problem-Solving Plan for Draw a Picture or Use a Model
(page 15)

Point out and review the Four-Step Problem-Solving Plan box at the top of the page.

Step 1

- Have students read the problem.

- Direct students to identify the question and important information in the problem.

- Have students answer the questions on the blackline master.

Step 2

- Ask students what steps they will take to solve the problem.

- Have students answer the questions on the blackline master.

Step 3

- Tell students to follow their plan to solve the problem.

- Make sure to tell students to show their work in the space provided on the blackline master.

Step 4

- Have students reread the problem to see if their answer makes sense.

- Tell students that to check their answer they can think of another way to solve the problem.

- Have students answer the question on the blackline master.

Draw a Picture or Use a Model

By drawing a picture or using a model, you can better understand the problem and what it is asking. When you draw a picture or use a model, you use information from the problem to show the problem in a different way.

Before You Solve

You should read the question and find the important information in the problem. Then, use this information to make a picture or a model.

How can a picture or model help you understand a solve a problem?

_____

_____

As You Solve

• After you read the problem, write the question being asked and important information in the chart.

• Think about whether drawing a picture or using a model will help you understand the information. Explain in the chart what you will do. Solve the problem.

• Copy and use this chart to help you solve other problems.

Problem Number	Question
Important Information	
Should I Draw a Picture or Use a Model?	
How Will This Help Me Solve the Problem?	

After You Solve

Look back at the problem you have solved and check your answer. How did your picture or model help you understand and solve the problem?

_____

The Four-Step Problem-Solving Plan for Draw a Picture or Use a Model

When you use the Four-Step Problem-Solving Plan, you decide what steps you will take to solve a problem.

THE FOUR-STEP PROBLEM-SOLVING PLAN

STEP 1: Read
STEP 2: Plan
STEP 3: Solve
STEP 4: Check

Step 1: Read

Read the problem and make sure you understand what it is asking. What is the question asking you to do?

_____

What information is in the problem that can help you answer the question?

_____

Step 2: Plan

Make a plan for how you will solve the problem. What will you do first?

_____

How will you complete the problem?

_____

_____

Step 3: Solve

Use the plan you made to solve the problem. Show your work.

Step 4: Check

Reread the problem and check that your answer makes sense. One way to check your answer is to think about another way to solve the problem. What other way can you solve this problem?

_____

_____

Find a Pattern

Patterns are everywhere: in number sequences, pictures, shapes, and words. Finding a pattern can help students solve problems in which numbers or objects repeat or change in a predictable way.

Here are some ways you can help your students apply the Four-Step Problem-Solving Plan with the Find a Pattern strategy to solve problems in science class.

1 Read

Students should read the problem to discover what information they are to gather. Students should study the problem to decide if they have all the information they need, and then begin thinking about the steps needed to solve the problem.

2 Plan

Students should think about the steps they will need to do to solve the problem. They will make a plan and lay out each step.

3 Solve

Students follow their plan to solve the problem.

4 Check

Students check their work and reread the problem to see if their answer makes sense.

Samples of how Find a Pattern can be used in science:

- Students learning about the periodic table of elements may learn about various patterns found in the table. For example, students may be asked to compare the atomic radius of two elements. Students may notice the pattern that atomic radius increases as you move from the top of the periodic table to the bottom. Elements in period 1 have electrons only in energy level 1. Period 2 elements begin to fill energy level 2, and so on. This pattern in atomic radius occurs because of the increasing number of energy levels holding electrons.

- Students learning about the number of petals on flowers, the number of branches or growing points on plants, and the arrangement of seeds in flower heads may notice that the numbers fit into a pattern called the Fibonacci sequence: 1, 1, 2, 3, 5, 8, 13, . . . In this sequence, to find the next term, you add the previous two terms.

Applying the Strategy: Find a Pattern

Here are some tips for helping students apply this strategy before, during, and after they solve problems:

Before Students Solve

- **Explain the strategy.** Say, *One way to solve problems is to look for a pattern. When you find a pattern, you see how numbers or objects repeat in a certain way. You try to find the "rule" of the pattern by seeing how numbers or objects relate to each other. Finding the "rule" will help you solve the problem.*

- **Model how to find a pattern.** Choose a science problem to solve. Say, *To solve this problem, I will look at the information in the problem to see if I can find a pattern. I will then find the "rule" of the pattern to see how it can help me solve the problem. In this problem...* (State the main question the problem is asking and identify the pattern. Then explain how to use the pattern to solve the problem.)

- **Evaluate a science problem with students.** Have students read a problem from their textbook and retell it in their own words. Next have them suggest how finding a pattern might help them understand the problem and solve it. (Copy and distribute page 19 as a guide to help students with this strategy.)

- **Have students check their understanding.** Direct students to stop periodically and ask themselves if they understand the problem they are working on. Have students summarize the problem.

As Students Solve

- **Have students check their understanding.** Direct students to stop periodically and ask themselves if they understand the problem they are working on. Have students identify the important information from the problem they can use to find a pattern.

- **Have students explain the pattern they found.** Ask volunteers to restate in their own words the main question the problem is asking. Then have them explain the pattern and its rule. Have them tell how the pattern helped them understand and solve the problem, so that students who are struggling can make a connection between finding a pattern and how to solve the problem.

After Students Solve

- **Have students check their work.** Then ask them to explain why their answer is correct.

- **If students' answers are not correct, have them reread the problem and make sure they correctly identified the pattern and its rule.** Help students use the pattern to get the correct answer.

Using the Blackline Masters

Students can use the blackline master on page 19 to practice the Find a Pattern strategy to help them solve problems. Have them use the blackline master on page 20 to practice the strategy with the Four-Step Problem-Solving Plan. Copy and distribute one or both blackline masters. Guide students through each part.

Find a Pattern
(page 19)

Before You Solve

- Provide students with a problem from a science text. Direct students to read the problem.

- Have students answer the questions on the blackline master and review their responses.

As You Solve

- Review the directions for the As You Solve chart.

- Guide students to identify the question being asked and important information in the problem. Have students identify the pattern, and have them explain how the rule of the pattern will help them solve the problem.

- Encourage students to copy the chart to help them solve other problems.

After You Solve

- Discuss the completed charts. Have students explain how they used the pattern to solve the problem.

- Have students respond to the After You Solve question and discuss.

The Four-Step Problem-Solving Plan for Find a Pattern
(page 20)

Point out and review the Four-Step Problem-Solving Plan box at the top of the page.

Step 1

- Have students read the problem.

- Direct students to identify the question and important information in the problem.

- Have students answer the questions on the blackline master.

Step 2

- Ask students what steps they will take to solve the problem.

- Have students answer the questions on the blackline master.

Step 3

- Tell students to follow their plan to solve the problem.

- Make sure to tell students to show their work in the space provided on the blackline master.

Step 4

- Have students reread the problem to see if their answer makes sense.

- Tell students that to check their answer they can think of another way to solve the problem.

- Have students answer the question on the blackline master.

Find a Pattern

Many problems can be solved by identifying a pattern. If you find the rule of the pattern you will be able to solve the problem.

Before You Solve

Read the problem and identify the important information. Can you find a pattern in the information?

_____

How can this pattern help you solve the problem?

_____

As You Solve

- After you read the problem, write the question being asked and important information in the chart.

- Try to find a pattern. Explain the rule of the pattern and complete the problem.

- Copy and use this chart to help you solve other problems.

Problem Number	Question
Important Information	
What is the pattern?	
What is the rule of the pattern?	

After You Solve

Look back at the problem you have solved and check your answer. How did finding a pattern help you understand and solve the problem?

_____

_____

The Four-Step Problem-Solving Plan for Find a Pattern

When you use the Four-Step Problem-Solving Plan, you decide what steps you will take to solve a problem.

> **THE FOUR-STEP PROBLEM-SOLVING PLAN**
> **STEP 1:** Read
> **STEP 2:** Plan
> **STEP 3:** Solve
> **STEP 4:** Check

Step 1: Read

Read the problem and make sure you understand what it is asking. What is the question asking you to do?

_____

What information is in the problem that can help you answer the question?

_____

Step 2: Plan

Make a plan for how you will solve the problem. What will you do first?

_____

How will you complete the problem?

_____

_____

Step 3: Solve

Use the plan you made to solve the problem. Show your work.

Step 4: Check

Reread the problem and check that your answer makes sense. One way to check your answer is to think about another way to solve the problem. What other way can you solve this problem?

_____

_____

Make a List

Students can make lists in order to see information in an organized way. When students make lists, they need to determine how they will organize the information. Lists can help students keep track of possible combinations of items or outcomes of situations.

Here are some ways you can help your students apply the Four-Step Problem-Solving Plan with the Make a List strategy to solve problems in science class.

1 Read

Students should read the problem to discover what information they are to gather. Students should study the problem to decide if they have all the information they need, and then begin thinking about the steps needed to solve the problem.

2 Plan

Students should think about the steps they will need to do to solve the problem. They will make a plan and lay out each step.

3 Solve

Students follow their plan to solve the problem.

4 Check

Students check their work and reread the problem to see if their answer makes sense.

Samples of how Make a List can be used in science:

- Students may be asked to classify certain plants or animals. To do this, students could list the features of the different plants or animals to determine how to classify them.

- Students may be asked to find all the possible outcomes for characteristics of offspring when two plants reproduce. For example, they may make a list by completing a Punnett square.

Applying the Strategy: Make a List

Here are some tips for helping students apply this strategy before, during, and after they solve problems:

Before Students Solve

- **Explain the strategy.** Say, *One way to solve problems is to make a list. Writing information down in an organized way can help you solve the problem.*

- **Model how to make a list.** Choose a science problem to solve. Say, *To solve this problem, I will look at the information in the problem and organize it in a list. In this problem...* (State the main question the problem is asking and identify what information is needed for the list. Then explain how to use the list to solve the problem.)

- **Evaluate a science problem with students.** Have students read a problem from their textbook and retell it in their own words. Next have them suggest how making a list might help them understand the problem and solve it. (Copy and distribute page 24 as a guide to help students with this strategy.)

As Students Solve

- **Have students check their understanding.** Direct students to stop periodically and ask themselves if they understand the problem they are working on. Have students identify the important information from the problem they can use to make a list.

- **Have students explain the lists they made.** Ask volunteers to restate in their own words the main question the problem is asking. Then have them explain their lists and how the list helps them solve the problem, so that students who are struggling can make a connection between making a list and how to solve the problem.

After Students Solve

- **Have students check their work.** Then ask them to explain why their answer is correct.

- **If students' answers are not correct, have them reread the problem and make sure their lists are complete.** Help students use the information in the list to get the correct answer.

Using the Blackline Masters

Students can use the blackline master on page 24 to practice the Make a List strategy to help them solve problems. Have them use the blackline master on page 25 to practice the strategy with the Four-Step Problem-Solving Plan. Copy and distribute one or both blackline masters. Guide students through each part.

Make a List
(page 24)

Before You Solve

- Provide students with a problem from a science text. Direct students to read the problem.

- Have students answer the question on the blackline master and review their responses.

As You Solve

- Review the directions for the As You Solve chart.

- Guide students to identify the question being asked and important information in the problem. Have students explain what information they used to make a list.

- Encourage students to copy the chart to help them solve other problems.

After You Solve

- Discuss the completed charts. Have students explain how they used the information in the list to solve the problem.

- Have students respond to the After You Solve question and discuss.

The Four-Step Problem-Solving Plan for Make a List
(page 25)

Point out and review the Four-Step Problem-Solving Plan box at the top of the page.

Step 1

- Have students read the problem.

- Direct students to identify the question and important information in the problem.

- Have students answer the questions on the blackline master.

Step 2

- Ask students what steps they will take to solve the problem.

- Have students answer the questions on the blackline master.

Step 3

- Tell students to follow their plan to solve the problem.

- Make sure to tell students to show their work in the space provided on the blackline master.

Step 4

- Have students reread the problem to see if their answer makes sense.

- Tell students that to check their answer they can think of another way to solve the problem.

- Have students answer the question on the blackline master.

Make a List

Organizing information in a list can help you solve problems. When you look at the information in your list, you can find the answer to the question.

Before You Solve

Read the problem and identify the important information. What information could you use to make a list?

_____

How can this list help you solve the problem?

_____

As You Solve

- After you read the problem, write the question being asked and important information in the chart.
- Then make a list with the information. Complete the problem.
- Copy and use this chart to help you solve other problems.

Problem Number	Question
Important Information	
List	

After You Solve

Look back at the problem you have solved and check your answer. How did making a list help you understand and solve the problem?

_____

_____

Name _____ Date _____

The Four-Step Problem-Solving Plan for Make a List

When you use the Four-Step Problem-Solving Plan, you decide what steps you will take to solve a problem.

THE FOUR-STEP PROBLEM-SOLVING PLAN

STEP 1: Read
STEP 2: Plan
STEP 3: Solve
STEP 4: Check

Step 1: Read

Read the problem and make sure you understand what it is asking. What is the question asking you to do?

_____

What information is in the problem that can help you answer the question?

_____

Step 2: Plan

Make a plan for how you will solve the problem. What will you do first?

_____

How will you complete the problem?

_____

_____

Step 3: Solve

Use the plan you made to solve the problem. Show your work.

Step 4: Check

Reread the problem and check that your answer makes sense. One way to check your answer is to think about another way to solve the problem. What other way can you solve this problem?

_____

_____

Try a Simpler Form of the Problem

Often, students are confronted with a difficult or complicated problem. Students can use prior knowledge about part of the problem to solve the whole problem. Students can also use simpler numbers to help them solve a complicated problem.

Here are some ways you can help your students apply the Four-Step Problem-Solving Plan with the Try a Simpler Form of the Problem strategy to solve problems in science class.

1 Read

Students should read the problem to discover what information they are to gather. Students should study the problem to decide if they have all the information they need, and then begin thinking about the steps needed to solve the problem.

2 Plan

Students should think about the steps they will need to do to solve the problem. They will make a plan and lay out each step.

3 Solve

Students follow their plan to solve the problem.

4 Check

Students check their work and reread the problem to see if their answer makes sense.

Samples of how Try a Simpler Form of the Problem can be used in science:

- Students may be asked to balance a long, difficult equation in chemistry. They may find it easier to think about what they know about balancing equations by using a shorter, simpler equation. They can then apply this practice and knowledge to the longer, more difficult equation.

- Students may encounter science problems that deal with very large numbers. Students can break the numbers down into smaller, more manageable numbers to work with and then use those results to solve the problem by using multiplication.

Applying the Strategy: Try a Simpler Form of the Problem

Here are some tips for helping students apply the strategy of summarizing before, during, and after they solve problems:

Before Students Solve

- **Explain the strategy.** Say, *One way to solve a complicated problem is to look for a part of the problem that you know how to solve and do that first. Then, move on to the rest of the problem. Another way to solve a complicated problem is to break large numbers into smaller numbers and then use multiplication to get the answer.*

- **Model how to solve a simpler form of the problem.** Choose a science problem to solve. Say, *To solve this problem, I will look at how I can break it into smaller, easier parts. I will then solve each part to get the answer to the problem. In this problem...* (State the main question the problem is asking and explain how you will make the problem simpler. Then explain how to solve the problem.)

- **Evaluate a science problem with students.** Have students read a problem from their textbook and retell it in their own words. Next have them suggest how making the problem simpler might help them solve it. (Copy and distribute page 29 as a guide to help students with this strategy.)

As Students Solve

- **Have students check their understanding.** Direct students to stop periodically and ask themselves if they understand the problem they are working on. Have students identify the important information in the problem and ask them how they could make the problem simpler.

- **Have students explain how they made the problem simpler.** Ask volunteers to restate in their own words the main question and problem is asking. Then have them explain how they used a simpler form to solve it. Point out that their may be more than one possible way to arrive at the correct answer.

- **Have students tell how using a simpler form helped them understand and solve the problem.** This will help students who are struggling to understand how using a simpler form of the problem can help them solve the problem.

- **Have students check their work.** Then ask them to explain why their answer is correct.

- **If students' answers are not correct, have them reread the problem and make sure they simplified the problem in a logical way.** Help students use the simpler form or parts to get the correct answer.

Using the Blackline Masters

Students can use the blackline master on page 29 to practice the Try a Simpler Form of the Problem strategy to help them solve problems. Have them use the blackline master on page 30 to practice the strategy with the Four-Step Problem-Solving Plan. Copy and distribute one or both blackline masters. Guide students through each part.

Try a Simpler Form of the Problem
(page 29)

Before You Solve
- Provide students with a problem from a science text. Direct students to read the problem.
- Have students answer the questions on the blackline master and review their responses.

As You Solve
- Review the directions for the As You Solve chart.
- Guide students to identify the question being asked and important information in the problem. Have students break the problem down into a simpler form, and have them explain how this will help them solve the problem.
- Encourage students to copy the chart to help them solve other problems.

After You Solve
- Discuss the completed charts. Have students explain how they used a simpler form to solve the problem.
- Have students respond to the After You Solve question and discuss.

The Four-Step Problem-Solving Plan for Try a Simpler Form of the Problem
(page 30)

Point out and review the Four-Step Problem-Solving Plan box at the top of the page.

Step 1
- Have students read the problem.
- Direct students to identify the question and important information in the problem.
- Have students answer the questions on the blackline master.

Step 2
- Ask students what steps they will take to solve the problem.
- Have students answer the questions on the blackline master.

Step 3
- Tell students to follow their plan to solve the problem.
- Make sure to tell students to show their work in the space provided on the blackline master.

Step 4
- Have students reread the problem to see if their answer makes sense.
- Tell students that to check their answer they can think of another way to solve the problem.
- Have students answer the question on the blackline master.

Try a Simpler Form of the Problem

To solve a difficult problem or a problem that uses complicated numbers, you can try to solve a simpler form of the problem.

Before You Solve

Read the problem and identify the important information. How can you make the problem simpler?

_____

How can the simpler form help you solve the problem?

_____

As You Solve

- After you read the problem, write the question being asked and important information in the chart.
- Try to break the problem into simpler parts or solve the problem using simpler numbers. Complete the problem.
- Copy and use this chart to help you solve other problems.

Problem Number	Question
Important Information	
Simpler Form	

After You Solve

Look back at the problem you have solved and check your answer. How did trying a simpler form of the problem help you understand and solve the problem?

_____

_____

The Four-Step Problem-Solving Plan for Try a Simpler Form of the Problem

When you use the Four-Step Problem-Solving Plan, you decide what steps you will take to solve a problem.

Step 1: Read

Read the problem and make sure you understand what it is asking. What is the question asking you to do?

_____

What information is in the problem that can help you answer the question?

_____

Step 2: Plan

Make a plan for how you will solve the problem. What will you do first?

_____

How will you complete the problem?

_____

_____

Step 3: Solve

Use the plan you made to solve the problem. Show your work.

Step 4: Check

Reread the problem and check that your answer makes sense. One way to check your answer is to think about another way to solve the problem. What other way can you solve this problem?

_____

_____

Make a Table or a Chart

Just as students can make lists in order to organize information, they can make tables or charts to organize and display information. Tables and charts can also be used to find patterns.

Here are some ways you can help your students apply the Four-Step Problem-Solving Plan with the Make a Table or a Chart strategy to solve problems in science class.

1 Read

Students should read the problem to discover what information they are to gather. Students should study the problem to decide if they have all the information they need, and then begin thinking about the steps needed to solve the problem.

2 Plan

Students should think about the steps they will need to do to solve the problem. They will make a plan and lay out each step.

3 Solve

Students follow their plan to solve the problem.

4 Check

Students check their work and reread the problem to see if their answer makes sense.

Samples of how Make a Table or a Chart can be used in science.

- Students may be asked to solve problems with a large amount of data. Arranging the data in a table or a chart can help them organize the information and solve the problem.

- Students often perform experiments in science classes in which they gather data. Making a table or a chart can help them record the data in an organized way and help them answer problems related to the experiment.

Applying the Strategy: Make a Table or a Chart

Here are some tips for helping students apply this strategy before, during, and after they solve problems:

Before Students Solve

- **Explain the strategy.** Say, *When solving problems that include a lot of information, or data, it is useful to make a table or a chart with that information. You can use the table or chart you make to help you solve the problem.*

- **Model how to solve a simpler form of the problem.** Choose a science problem to solve. Say, *To solve this problem, I will look at the information provided and see how I can use that information to make a table or a chart. I will then use my table or chart to answer the problem. In this problem...* (State the main question the problem is asking and explain how you will use data from the problem to make a table or a chart. Then explain how to use the table or chart to solve the problem.)

- **Evaluate a science problem with students.** Have students read a problem from their textbook and retell it in their own words. Next have them suggest how making a table or a chart might help them solve it. (Copy and distribute page 34 as a guide to help students with this strategy.)

As Students Solve

- **Have students check their understanding.** Direct students to stop periodically and ask themselves if they understand the problem they are working on. Have students identify the important information in the problem and ask them how they could make a table or a chart using this information.

- **Have students explain the charts or tables they made.** Ask volunteers to restate in their own words the main question the problem is asking. Then have them explain what information from the problem they used to make a table or a chart. Point out that there may be more than one possible way to show the information to arrive at the correct answer.

- **Have students tell how making a table or a chart helped them understand and solve the problem.** This will help students who are struggling to understand how making a table or a chart connects to solving the problem.

After Students Solve

- **Have students check their work.** Then ask them to explain why their answer is correct.

- **If students' answers are not correct, have them reread the problem and make sure their table or chart is accurate.** Help students use the information in their table or chart to get the correct answer.

Using the Blackline Masters

Students can use the blackline master on page 34 to practice the Make a Table or a Chart strategy to help them solve problems. Have them use the blackline master on page 35 to practice the strategy with the Four-Step Problem-Solving Plan. Copy and distribute one or both blackline masters. Guide students through each part.

Make a Table or a Chart
(page 34)

Before You Solve
- Provide students with a problem from a science text. Direct students to read the problem.

- Have students answer the questions on the blackline master and review their responses.

As You Solve
- Review the directions for the As You Solve chart.

- Guide students to identify the question being asked and important information in the problem. Have students decide how to use the information in a table or a chart and have them explain how this will help them solve the problem.

- Encourage students to copy the chart to help them solve other problems.

After You Solve
- Discuss the completed charts. Have students explain how they used a table or a chart to solve the problem.

- Have students respond to the After You Solve question and discuss.

The Four-Step Problem-Solving Plan for Make a Table or a Chart
(page 35)

Point out and review the Four-Step Problem-Solving Plan box at the top of the page.

Step 1
- Have students read the problem.

- Direct students to identify the question and important information in the problem.

- Have students answer the questions on the blackline master.

Step 2
- Ask students what steps they will take to solve the problem.

- Have students answer the questions on the blackline master.

Step 3
- Tell students to follow their plan to solve.

- Make sure to tell students to show their work in the space provided on the blackline master.

Step 4
- Have students reread the problem to see if their answer makes sense.

- Tell students that to check their answer they can think of another way to solve the problem.

- Have students answer the question on the blackline master.

Make a Table or a Chart

To solve a problem that has a lot of information, or data, you can make a table or a chart to organize the information. Then, use your table or chart to help you solve the problem.

Before You Solve

Read the problem and identify the important information. What information can you use to make a table or a chart?

_____

How can a table or a chart help you solve the problem?

_____

As You Solve

- After you read the problem, write the question being asked and important information in the chart.
- Then draw a table or a chart using the important information. Complete the problem.
- Copy and use this chart to help you solve other problems.

Problem Number	Question
Important Information	
Table or Chart	

After You Solve

Look back at the problem you have solved and check your answer. How did making a table or a chart help you understand and solve the problem?

_____

_____

The Four-Step Problem-Solving Plan for Make a Table or a Chart

When you use the Four-Step Problem-Solving Plan, you decide what steps you will take to solve a problem.

Step 1: Read

Read the problem and make sure you understand what it is asking. What is the question asking you to do?

_____

What information is in the problem that can help you answer the question?

_____

Step 2: Plan

Make a plan for how you will solve the problem. What will you do first?

_____

How will you complete the problem?

_____

_____

Step 3: Solve

Use the plan you made to solve the problem. Show your work.

Step 4: Check

Reread the problem and check that your answer makes sense. One way to check your answer is to think about another way to solve the problem. What other way can you solve this problem?

_____

_____

Guess, Check, and Revise

Students can use this strategy to make a logical guess about the answer to a problem, check their work, and revise their answer as necessary. There are many instances where making a prediction or guessing and then revising that answer can be useful in the problem-solving process.

Here are some ways you can help your students apply the Four-Step Problem-Solving Plan with the Guess, Check, and Revise strategy to solve problems in science class.

1 Read

Students should read the problem to discover what information they are to gather. Students should study the problem to decide if they have all the information they need, and then begin thinking about the steps needed to solve the problem.

2 Plan

Students should think about the steps they will need to do to solve the problem. They will make a plan and lay out each step.

3 Solve

Students follow their plan to solve the problem.

4 Check

Students check their work and reread the problem to see if their answer makes sense.

Samples of how Guess, Check, and Revise can be used in science:

- The Guess, Check, and Revise strategy is very similar to the scientific method which includes forming a hypothesis and experimenting to either prove or disprove that hypothesis.

- Students may encounter problems in which it seems there are several possible answers. For example, students may be looking for an amount of an element that will correctly balance a chemical equation. They may need to start by choosing an amount, checking if it is reasonable, and then adjusting based on what they learn until they arrive at the correct answer.

Applying the Strategy: Guess, Check, and Revise

Here are some tips for helping students apply this strategy before, during, and after they solve problems:

Before Students Solve

- **Explain the strategy.** Say, *When solving a problem, you can often start with a reasonable guess, evaluate that guess, and work your way to the correct answer.*

- **Model how to use the Guess, Check, and Revise strategy.** Choose a science problem to solve. Say, *To solve this problem, I will use the information given to make a reasonable guess about what I think the answer could be. Then, I will check to see if my answer works. If it doesn't, I'll revise my answer and continue checking until I arrive at the correct answer. In this problem...* (State the main question the problem is asking and the details that are necessary to solve it.)

- **Evaluate a science problem with students.** Have students read a problem from their textbook and retell it in their own words. Next have them suggest how first making a reasonable guess might help them solve the problem. (Copy and distribute page 39 as a guide to help students with this strategy.)

As Students Solve

- **Have students check their understanding.** Direct students to stop periodically and ask themselves if they understand the problem they are working on. Have students identify the important information from the problem and how they can use that information to make an informed guess at the answer.

- **Have students explain why they made their first guess.** Ask volunteers to restate in their own words the main question and problem is asking. Then have them tell what information they used to make their guess. Have them explain how they checked this guess and revised as necessary to get the correct answer, so that students who are struggling can make a connection between the first guess and eventual result of the correct answer.

After Students Solve

- **Have students check their work.** Then ask them to explain why their answer is correct.

- **If students' answers are not correct, have them reread the problem and make sure they identified the important information, made logical guesses, and revised their guesses correctly.** Help students use the revised guesses to arrive at the correct answer.

Using the Blackline Masters

Students can use the blackline master on page 39 to practice the Guess, Check, and Revise strategy to help them solve problems. Have them use the blackline master on page 40 to practice the strategy with the Four-Step Problem-Solving Plan. Copy and distribute one or both blackline masters. Guide students through each part.

Guess, Check, and Revise
(page 39)

Before You Solve

- Provide students with a problem from a science text. Direct students to read the problem.

- Have students answer the question on the blackline master and review their responses.

As You Solve

- Review the directions for the As You Solve chart.

- Guide students to identify the question being asked and important information in the problem. Have students use the information to make a reasonable guess, and check it. Then have them explain how this guess may need to be revised to help them solve the problem.

- Encourage students to copy the chart to help them solve other problems.

After You Solve

- Discuss the completed charts. Have students share the guess, check, and revise process they used to solve the problem.

- Explain that although some students may have begun with different guesses, the process eventually lead to the same answer.

- Have students respond to the After You Solve question and discuss.

The Four-Step Problem-Solving Plan for Guess, Check, and Revise
(page 40)

Point out and review the Four-Step Problem-Solving Plan box at the top of the page.

Step 1

- Have students read the problem.

- Direct students to identify the question and important information in the problem.

- Have students answer the questions on the blackline master.

Step 2

- Ask students what steps they will take to solve.

- Have students answer the questions on the blackline master.

Step 3

- Tell students to follow their plan to solve.

- Make sure to tell students to show their work in the space provided on the blackline master.

Step 4

- Have students reread the problem to see if their answer makes sense.

- Tell students that to check their answer they can think of another way to solve the problem.

- Have students answer the question on the blackline master.

Guess, Check, and Revise

When solving a problem, you can often use information given in the problem to make a reasonable guess about the answer. Then, you check your guess. If it is not correct, revise it until you get the correct answer.

Before You Solve

Read the question and find the important information. Then, make a reasonable guess about the answer. Check your guess.

How can making a reasonable guess and checking it help you solve a problem?

———————————————————————————————————

———————————————————————————————————

As You Solve

- After you read the problem, write the question being asked and important information in the chart.

- Think about how you can use this information to make a guess. In the chart, write down your guess. Check your guess and revise if you need to. Solve the problem.

- Copy and use this chart to help you solve other problems.

Problem Number	Question
Important Information	
First Guess	
Check	
How I Found the Correct Answer	

After You Solve

Look back at the problem you have solved and the work you did to check your guesses. How did the Guess, Check, and Revise strategy help you solve the problem?

———————————————————————————————————

Name _____   Date _____

The Four-Step Problem-Solving Plan for Guess, Check, and Revise

When you use the Four-Step Problem-Solving Plan, you decide what steps you will take to solve a problem.

THE FOUR-STEP PROBLEM-SOLVING PLAN
STEP 1: Read
STEP 2: Plan
STEP 3: Solve
STEP 4: Check

Step 1: Read

Read the problem and make sure you understand what it is asking. What is the question asking you to do?

_____

What information is in the problem that can help you answer the question?

_____

Step 2: Plan

Make a plan for how you will solve the problem. What will you do first?

_____

How will you complete the problem?

_____

_____

Step 3: Solve

Use the plan you made to solve the problem. Show your work.

Step 4: Check

Reread the problem and check that your answer makes sense. One way to check your answer is to think about another way to solve the problem. What other way can you solve this problem?

_____

_____

Graphic Organizers

Concept Map

Use with

- Draw a Picture or Use a Model

- Make a List

Tip: Draw more outer sections as needed.

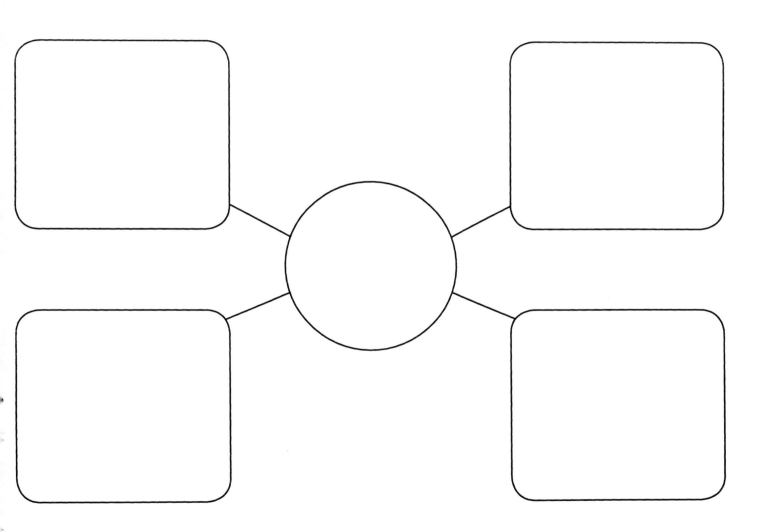

Graphic Organizers

Venn Diagram

Use with

- Draw a Picture or Use a Model
- Make a List

Tip: Write the similarities where the circles overlap and the differences in the outer parts of the circles.

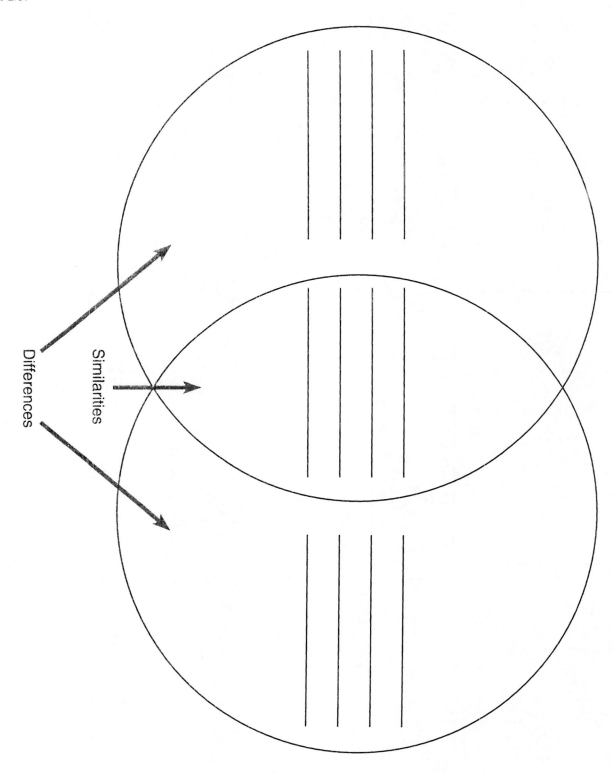

Graphic Organizers

Flowchart

Use with

- The Four-Step Problem-Solving Plan
- Guess, Check, and Revise

Tip: Add more boxes as needed to include more steps or events.

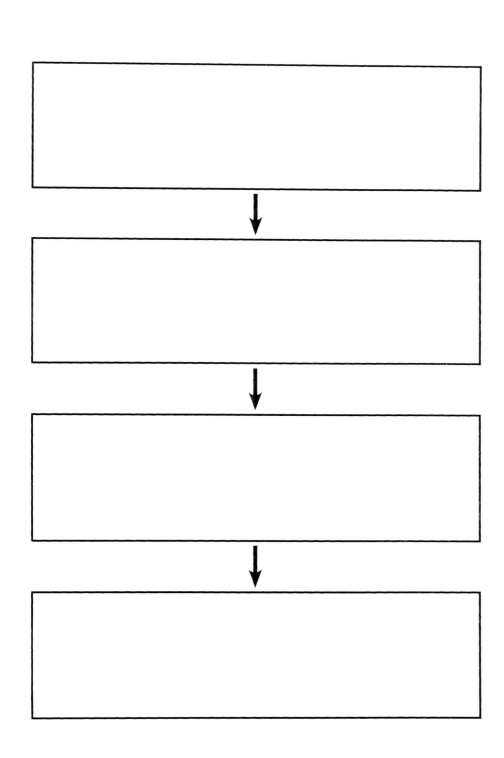

Graphic Organizers

Three-Column Chart

Use with

- Make a List
- Find a Pattern
- Make a Table or a Chart

Tip: Label each column.

Graphic Organizers

Bar Graph

Use with

- Draw a Picture or Use a Model
- Make a Table or a Chart

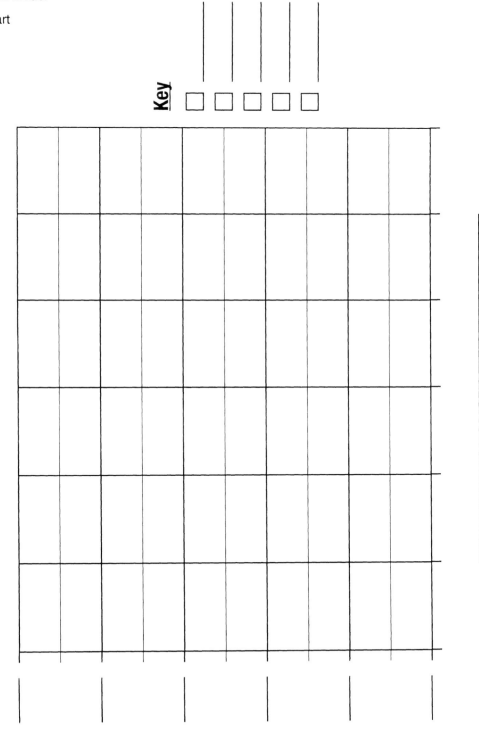

Graphic Organizers

Circle Graph

Use with

- Draw a Picture or Use a Model
- Make a Table or a Chart

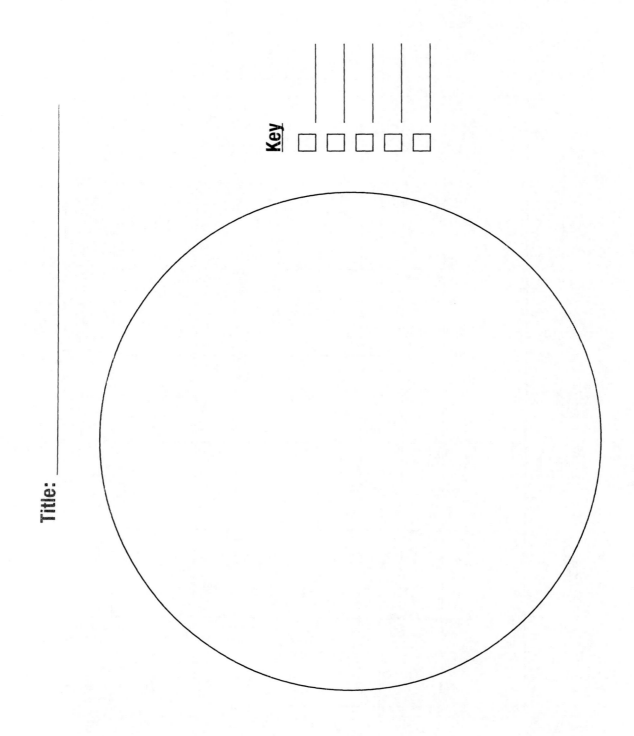

Key

Title:

Graphic Organizers

Coordinate Grid

Use with

- Draw a Picture or Use a Model
- Make a Table or a Chart

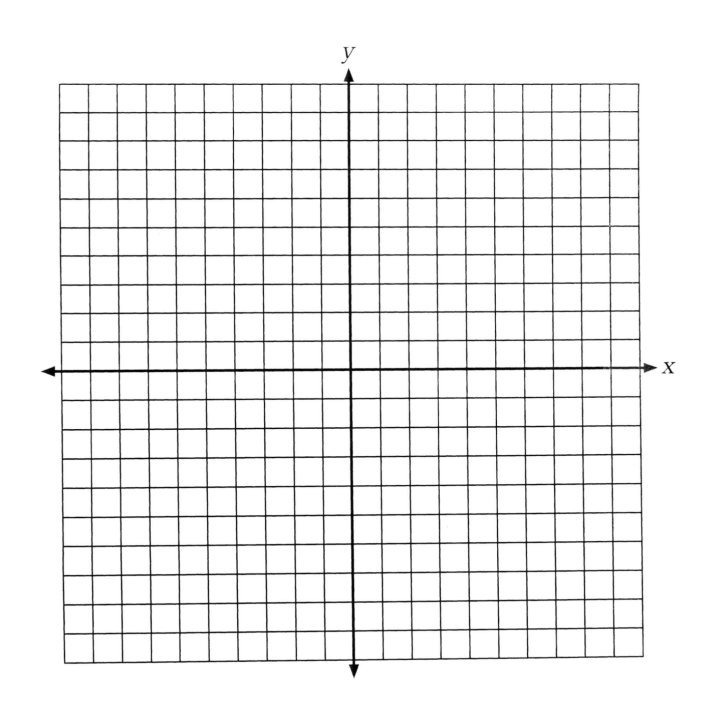